4-98

②

12-98 gm

6 in HT

SCIENTIFIC
AMERICAN **SOURCEBOOKS**

POISONOUS
CREATURES

NATHAN AASENG

TWENTY-FIRST CENTURY BOOKS

A Division of Henry Holt and Company
New York

Twenty-First Century Books / A Division of Henry Holt and Company, Inc. / *Publishers since 1866*
115 West 18th Street / New York, NY 10011

Henry Holt® and colophon are trademarks of Henry Holt and Company, Inc.

Henry Holt and Company, Inc., and Scientific American, Inc., are both wholly owned subsidiaries of Holtzbrinck Publishing Holdings Limited Partnership. Twenty-First Century Books, a division of Henry Holt and Company, Inc., is using the Scientific American name under a special license with that company.

Published in Canada by Fitzhenry & Whiteside Ltd.
195 Allstate Parkway, Markham, Ontario, L3R 4T8

The map featured in this book was created by Mark Stein.

Library of Congress Cataloging-in-Publication Data
Aaseng, Nathan / Poisonous creatures / Nathan Aaseng.
p. cm.—(Scientific American sourcebooks)
Includes bibliographical references (p.   ) and index.
Summary: Describes various species from every animal family that use some
kind of venom to protect themselves or as a means of acquiring food.
1. Poisonous animals—Juvenile literature.   [1. Poisonous animals.]   I. Title.   II. Series.
QL100.A37   1997   591.6'5—dc21   97-8728
ISBN 0-8050-4690-9
First Edition 1997

Printed in Mexico on acid-free paper ∞.
10 9 8 7 6 5 4 3 2 1

Photo Credits
pp. 4, 47 (all), 78: © Mark Moffett/Minden Pictures; pp. 12, 20 (i   26, 30 (inset): © Norbert Wu; p. 13: © Ben Cropp/Mo Yung Productions; p. 16: © Kat   kinson/Oxford Scientific Films/Animals Animals; p. 16 (inset): © Peter Parks/Mo Yung   ctions; p. 17: © David B. Fleetham/Visuals Unlimited; p. 20: © Rodie H. Kuiter/Oxford S   fic Films/Animals Animals; pp. 22 (all), 23: © Alex Kerstitch/Visuals Unlimited; p. 28:   ed McConnaughey/Photo Researchers, Inc.; p. 30: © Hal Beral/Visuals Unlimited; p. 31: ©   Yamamoto/Woodfin Camp; p. 31 (inset): © Ken Lucas/Visuals Unlimited; p 34: © Gerry   ENP Images; p. 35: © Tom McHugh/Photo Researchers, Inc.; p. 37: © John Serrao/Photo   chers, Inc.; p. 39: © Dr. H.S. Banton, Jr./Photo Researchers, Inc.; p. 41: © Doug Sokell/Visu   limited; p. 41 (inset): © E. R. Degginger/Animals Animals; p. 45: © Scott Camazine/Photo   archers, Inc.; p. 48: © Science VU/Visuals Unlimited; p. 49: © J. H. Robinson/Photo Researchers, Inc.; p. 50: © Michael Fogden/Animals Animals; p. 54: © Cancalo/Tom Stack & Associates; p. 58 (both): © Renee Lynn/Photo Researchers, Inc.; p. 59: © Brian Parker/Tom Stack & Associates; p. 65: © Breck Kent/Animals Animals; pp. 63, 66, 67, 76: © William B. Love; p. 70: © Stephen Kraseman/Photo Researchers, Inc.; p. 72: © Craig K. Lorenz/Photo Researchers, Inc.; p. 74: © W. Peckover/VIREO; p. 76 (inset): © A. J. Stevens/Animals Animals.

CONTENTS

*P*oison dart frog

INTRODUCTION

POISON IN NATURE

A huge python slithers silently through the water toward its prey—a shorebird known as a plover. With a lightning quick lunge, the snake snatches the unsuspecting bird. It coils its thick, muscular body around the thrashing plover and begins to squeeze the life out of it. In a frantic attempt to escape, however, the plover slashes the python with the sharp spur on its wing, dealing a fatal blow.

Meanwhile, a small viper lies in wait along a grassy path as a rat approaches. The snake is only a fraction of the size of the python. It has nowhere near the overwhelming superiority in strength that the python held over the plover. Yet, while the python lies dying, the viper kills and eats the rat without suffering so much as a scratch from a claw or tooth.

The viper possesses one advantage not available to the python—a supply of venom or poison. Venom is a substance made up of complex proteins that produces destructive chemical reactions when it comes into contact with an animal. The viper could avoid dangerous physical contact by striking quickly, injecting venom, and then retreating out of harm's way while the venom finished the kill.

CHEMICAL WARFARE   The kind of chemical warfare employed by the viper has proven enormously effective over the centuries. Virtually every animal family includes species that pack poison in order to survive. From tiny beetles to 18-foot (5.5-meter) long cobras, from docile sponges to swarming bees, the animal world contains arsenals of venom. Venomous animals have invaded every habitat from the ocean depths to mountain peaks, from scorching deserts to steamy rain forests and the frigid lands above the Arctic Circle.

Poison serves two major purposes in the animal world. The most obvious is to help predators acquire their meals. Poison does this by either immobilizing or killing animals that would otherwise escape from the predator or harm it while defending themselves.

A predator can use venom for this purpose only if it has some way of injecting the venom into the prey. Most venomous predators have specially adapted teeth to pierce the prey's skin. Venom glands located near the teeth send poison flowing, either through hollow teeth or along grooves in the teeth, into the prey. Other predators have developed stingers at the end of their tails or on dangling tentacles to inject their poison.

Venom is useful to a predator only if the predator has some way of getting close enough to the prey to inject the poison, even if only for a fraction of a second. A few hunting spiders, scorpions, and snakes have the speed, agility, and endurance to run down their prey in the open. Other venomous predators target slow-moving or stationary prey, such as baby mammals and birds.

But most venomous predators resort to either trapping or ambushing unsuspecting prey. Spiders are well known for building webs to ensnare the insects they eat. Some snakes trap their prey in burrows, and certain sea snakes corner their intended meals in crevices and against coral reefs. Many snakes dig into sand, lie hidden in debris, or are covered in patterns and colors that allow them to blend with their surroundings. Most spiders and scorpions lurk in shadows and corners, waiting for prey to happen by. Jellyfish have nearly transparent tentacles that dangle in the water, ready to snare fish that blunder into them.

POISON DEFENSES   The second main purpose for poison in animals is for protection. Some animals defend themselves by actively injecting their venom into their attackers, just as predators do. Wasps and stingrays are well-known examples of animals that inject poison in self-defense.

Other creatures are passively poisonous. Poison dart frogs, for example, have no way of injecting their highly toxic skin secretions into attacking birds or bats. But their toxins can disable and even kill animals that try to eat them.

Some animals use poison for both predation and for defense. The stinging cells of a jellyfish not only help the animal to gather food but also discourage other animals from harming it. Many poisonous snakes use venom not only to subdue prey but also to fight off intruders that threaten them.

Sometimes the poison protects the individual animal, as in the case of a cornered snake. At other times, however, the poison is of no use to the individual, but it helps defend other members of the species. For example, a honeybee's venomous sting does not protect it; in fact, the act of stinging causes its death. But its action serves to protect the hive from danger. A caterpillar's poisonous secretions may not begin to take effect until after the creature is killed. But a bird that experiences the burning or foul-tasting sensation caused by the caterpillar may learn to avoid those types of caterpillars in the future. In such a case, the poison reduces the chances that other members of the species will be attacked.

ATTENTION: POISON!

Unlike most animals, whose behavior and coloration help them avoid detection, poisonous prey animals often call attention to themselves. Poison dart frogs, for example, display some of the boldest, splashiest colors found in nature. Poisonous prey that are easily recognizable run less risk of attack by predators who remember painful encounters with similar creatures. The bright colors are, in effect, advertisements to the rest of the world. They warn potential predators not to mess with this animal because it is poisonous.

Occasionally, even venomous predators find advantages in calling attention to themselves. A rattlesnake lying in ambush for a small prey animal must be able to blend with its surroundings. Its coloration and mottled patterns help it to do so. However, blending with surroundings can be a problem for a rattlesnake when large animals such as horses and humans approach because they could accidentally step on it. Although a rattlesnake can protect itself by biting, it has nothing to gain and much to lose by fighting a large animal. Therefore, it shakes its rattles to alert large creatures to its presence and to warn them away.

HOW POISON WORKS

Animal venom comes in two general varieties. Most poisonous animals use neurotoxins—poisons that damage the nervous system. These chemicals disrupt the nerve messages to vital organs such as the heart and lungs. Death often results from asphyxiation, the stoppage of breathing; or from cardiac arrest, the stoppage of the heart.

The other main type of poisons are the hemotoxins, which act on blood cells and tissue. These toxins may cause internal bleeding, prevent blood from clotting, or may cause excessive blood clotting. Because they destroy muscle and other types of tissue, they tend to produce more damage to a specific area of the body than do neurotoxins and can leave scars.

Venom usually works most effectively against the particular prey that the predator most often eats. Researchers have found, for example, that the toxin of one species of mammal-eating snake is 100 times more effective against the small rodents it usually eats than against lizards it rarely preys on.

Medical researchers have been able to counter the effect of venom in the human body by developing antivenin (see the Conclusion). Specific types of antivenin work against specific venom; there is no universal antivenin that works against all animal venom. Some animals produce venom for which no effective antivenin has been developed. Others produce venom that contains both hemotoxins and neurotoxins. Victims of these animals may need to be treated with a combination of antivenins. Antivenin is expensive to produce. A single dose may cost from $25 to $1,000.

POISONOUS CREATURES AND HUMANS Of the vast store of venom found in the animal world, very little is intended for use against humans. No venomous animals target humans as prey. Nevertheless, the venom of many animals is dangerously effective against humans. While there has never been a reliable world tally of incidents involving people and animal poison, hundreds of thousands of people die from these encounters every year. University of Arizona professor Findlay Russell estimates that snakebites alone kill close to 100,000 people throughout the world each year, although other experts put the figure closer to 40,000. Among an Ecuadorian tribe known as the Waorani, snakebite causes nearly 5 of every 100 deaths.

Yet venomous animals are not so widespread and dangerous that humans need to live in constant fear of them. By learning about the habits and identifying markings of poisonous animals and by using common sense and caution, humans can safely share the outdoors with poisonous creatures in most habitats.

~~~~~~~~~~~~~~~~~~~~~~~~~~~~~~~~~~~

ONE

SEA CREATURES WITH STINGING CELLS

For many years vacationers enjoying a summer swim in the Pacific Ocean off the coast of northeast Australia dreaded a mysterious attacker. All had heard tales of swimmers bursting out of the water, shrieking in agony. Angry welts that looked like terrible rope burns blistered the swimmers' skin. In many cases, the victim died within minutes. Neither the victim nor other observers in the water ever saw what sort of creature had made the attack.

SEA WASPS   Not until 1956 did marine scientists identify the culprit—a box jellyfish, also called a sea wasp. Based on appearance, this animal seems out of place on a roster of the deadly predators of the world such as sharks, cobras, or tigers. The main body of the sea wasp is only about the size of a cantaloupe. It is soft and squishy—about 95 percent water. The box-shaped creature moves too slowly to pounce on any prey.

Yet, according to Australian physician Peter Fenner, who has treated victims of this animal, the sea wasp "is without question the most venomous animal on earth."

Lethal Harpoons   The deadly sea wasp is actually just the sexual stage of an animal with a complicated life cycle. During the summer, adult sea wasps gather in the shallow waters and river mouths off the coast of northeastern Australia. Late in the summer, just before they die, they produce young in the form of microscopic balls of cells called planulae. These planulae settle on the bottom of the ocean where they grow into small organisms called polyps. The polyps, which attach themselves to rocks, look like mushroom stems with a ring of tentacles on top. In the spring the polyps change into medusa, the venomous, free-floating adult form of the sea wasp.

Sea wasps are members of a group of animals called the cnidaria. (The *c* is silent.) These animals all have specialized nerve cells that form capsules called nematocysts. Nematocysts are filled with long, coiled threads that end in sharp, barbed points. They are equipped with bristles that can detect chemicals and alert the nematocyst to the presence of other animals nearby. When that happens, the nematocyst opens and the barbed filament springs out and pricks the animal. There is no avoiding a triggered nematocyst, which fires at 10,000 times the acceleration of a rocket launched into space!

The nematocysts of the sea wasp are located on about five dozen tentacles that hang down in clusters from the corners of the sea wasp's body. These tentacles are only a quarter of an inch (6 millimeters) thick and almost invisible, particularly when the water is murky.

The sea wasp can propel itself through the water at a rate of a few feet

A sea wasp polyp eats tiny prey, such as brine shrimp.

Nematocysts on its tentacles make the sea wasp a tremendously dangerous animal.

per second. Amazingly, despite the fact that sea wasps do not have a brain, experiments have shown that the animals appear to be able to see certain objects. Nevertheless, the sea wasp is not an active hunter that seeks out and attacks its prey. Instead, it floats with its tentacles acting like fishing lines as they extend as far as 20 feet (6 meters) beneath the sea wasp. Prey blunder into the tentacles.

Concentrated Toxin   The sea wasp does not waste its lethal poison on just any creature that happens by. Its nematocysts will only fire if stimulated by a chemical that is given off by its primary food: fish and shellfish. The danger to humans comes from the unfortunate coincidence that humans also give off that same chemical.

Each nematocyst contains a microscopic drop made up of two types of incredibly potent neurotoxin. Even diluted 10,000 times, this venom can

---

⌁ PANTYHOSE TO THE RESCUE ⌁

Sea wasps are a menace during the summer months in Australia because they float in the shallow water off the country's most popular beaches, where shrimp and small fish are plentiful. Anyone swimming unprotected off the coast of northeast Australia during this time is asking for trouble. Sea wasp accidents are rare, but at least five dozen deaths have been reported in the past century. The toxin slows the heartbeat and rate of breathing so dramatically that death can occur in as little as 30 seconds. Even the slightest brush with a sea wasp causes instant, unbearable agony.

Swimmers have discovered an unusual armor to protect themselves from the sea wasp's deadly sting—pantyhose. The barbed stingers of the sea wasp are so tiny that they can barely penetrate human skin. A layer of material as thin as nylon pantyhose can block the stingers from entering. A full body suit, such as the suits skin divers wear, provides even more reliable protection. Australia also uses mesh fences in the water to provide enclosed, safe areas for swimming.

Until 1970 physicians were unable to do much to help victims of sea wasp accidents. Since then, medical researchers have developed an antivenin that can restore normal breathing and relieve pain if administered immediately.

kill small laboratory animals. A single sea wasp contains enough poison to kill 60 humans.

Nematocysts are so small that even with this powerful poison, a single nematocyst's sting would not be noticeable. But scientists estimate that the sea wasp packs as many as a half million of these stinging cells *per square inch (6.2 square centimeters)*! When several feet worth of these cells fire all at once, the effect can be devastating. A total of about 10 feet (3 meters) of tentacle must make contact with human skin to deliver a fatal dose.

The sea wasp's venom usually kills its prey instantly. The tentacles then reel in the prey to the sea wasp's body. There, special cells digest the sea wasp's latest meal.

Why does the sea wasp need such an overpowering venom? Perhaps because it is such a fragile creature. The sea wasp is a loose collection of cells with no bones, shell, or even tough skin to hold it together or protect it. A single flip of a small fish's tail could shred several feet of tentacles and slice open the body. A fish thrashing around in its death throes for several seconds could easily destroy the sea wasp. Powerful venom that produces instant death protects the sea wasp from any such damaging struggles.

PORTUGUESE MAN-OF-WAR   The most famous poisonous creature of the Atlantic Ocean is the Portuguese man-of-war. Legend has it that, hundreds of years ago, English sailors spotted a fleet of these floating gasbags off the coast of Portugal. The creatures reminded the sailors of miniature warships, so they gave them their common name of Portuguese man-of-war.

In a way, a Portuguese man-of-war *is* a warship—a sailing vessel that can fire hundreds of thousands of tiny weapons. A single, overgrown polyp forms a purplish-blue bag, roughly a foot in diameter, with a flexible crest. (The animals' scientific name *Physalia* comes from the Greek word for "bladder.") Filled with carbon monoxide gas, the bag tilts from side to side so that both sides frequently dip into the water. This keeps the bag from drying out. Like the sails of a ship, the bladder catches the breeze at an angle, propelling the creature across the water. Man-of-wars are most numerous in warm waters near the Caribbean Sea and in the shallow Sargasso Sea in the mid-Atlantic. They often sail along with the current into the North Atlantic and then eastward, occasionally to the Mediterranean Sea.

The inset photograph shows unfired nematocysts of a Portuguese man-of-war.

Like the sea wasp, the man-of-war has polyps that form fishing tentacles loaded with stinging cells, and others that perform digestive and reproductive functions. But because the man-of-war does not survive in captivity, scientists know little about its habits.

Deadly Fishing Lines

The man-of-war's tentacles are much longer than those of the sea wasp—they may extend over 100 feet (30 meters) into the ocean. While the creature's neurotoxin is not as deadly as the sea wasp's, it is strong enough to instantly kill most small fish. After making a kill, the tentacles contract and reel in the fish to the digestive cells. These cells secrete enzymes that break down the proteins in the prey.

The man-of-war does not have to kill and eat its prey one at a time. While one tentacle is contracting with its prey, the others remain poised for more action. A man-of-war may catch and eat two dozen fish at once.

These creatures can inflict painful and possibly lethal injuries on humans. The tentacles stick to the skin and shoot tiny darts of poison all along the contact area. A Portuguese man-of-war can keep stinging long after it is dead. Stringy, dried blue tentacles of man-of-wars washed up on beaches have caused numerous painful wounds and left scars on unsuspecting beachcombers. The venom has been frozen and stored for up to six years without losing its potency.

Poison Doesn't Guarantee Respect   You might expect that all creatures of the ocean would be careful to avoid the stinging-celled hunters of the sea world. On the contrary, even the deadly sea wasp is as much the hunted as it is the hunter. A number of creatures are immune to the poison of sea wasps and the Portuguese man-of-war and so have no reason to fear them.

The nomeus, or man-of-war fish, hides among the jellyfish's tentacles—hoping to snatch a meal, or escape from predators.

Loggerhead turtles, for example, make a meal of these creatures whenever they get a chance. These 500-pound (230-kilogram) reptiles can swim right through a cluster of stinging tentacles, slashing and devouring as they go, with no apparent effect. The ocean sunfish is another predator of poisonous jellyfish.

Some animals actually steal the jellyfishs' poison. Tiny sea creatures known as nudibranchs feed on Portuguese man-of-war tentacles. They are able to extract the nematocysts without triggering them and transfer them to their own bodies. This allows the nudibranchs to sting other animals. One kind of octopus breaks tentacles off the Portuguese man-of-war and has been known to use these tentacles to sting other creatures.

Although one certain type of fish does not kill man-of-wars, it takes such advantage of them that it is commonly called the man-of-war fish. The man-of-war fish swims among the tentacles and snatches fish already killed by the man-of-war's stingers. When chased by predators, this blue and silver-banded fish darts behind the man-of-war's tentacles for protection.

Marine biology professor Charles Lane of the University of Miami subjected the man-of-war fish to ten times the amount of Portuguese man-of-war toxin needed to kill an average fish its size. According to Lane, "The little scavengers swam away as if nothing had happened."

SEA ANEMONES   Sea anemones are another group of cnidarians that can pack a toxic wallop. These small, fleshy, plantlike creatures come in a variety of bright colors. Unlike sea wasps and the man-of-war, anemones do not float around in the water. Instead, they anchor themselves to rocks and other objects. They can be found almost anywhere in the ocean, even down to the murky depths 30,000 feet (9,200 meters) below the surface.

Some anemones are simply filter-feeders who trap tiny animals and particles of suspended food in their sticky tentacles. Others actively catch small crustaceans and fish in sticky threads. Their nematocysts are not as potent as those of the jellyfish. Humans have nothing to fear from most anemones, which inflict only a minor reaction, at worst, on humans. However, there's a bright orange Pacific species that can cause painful stings.

TWO

MOLLUSKS

The soft-bodied group of creatures called mollusks does not generally rank among the most feared poisonous animals. Mollusks include octopus, squid, snails, and clams, none of which have a strong reputation for venom.

BLUE-RINGED OCTOPUS   But experienced sea divers know better than to fool around with the blue-ringed octopus. This tiny eight-armed creature, only 6 to 8 inches (15 to 21 centimeters) across from armtip to armtip, is easily identified by the bright blue rings on its brownish body.

The blue-ringed octopus lives in shallow water along the southeastern coast of Australia. It hides in rock crevices and ocean debris, waiting for crabs, small fish, and other marine animals to wander close. When prey draws within striking distance, the octopus grabs it from behind and bites it with its hard, parrotlike beak.

The blue-ringed octopus's mouth contains a type of venomous neurotoxin produced in large salivary glands. This toxin enters the prey through the bite wound and quickly takes effect as it interferes with the prey's nerve messages. The prey suffers paralysis and respiratory failure.

The toxin of the blue-ringed octopus is lethal to humans. An average specimen may produce enough venom to kill 10 people. Its bite is so quick and painless that most humans are not aware when a bite occurs. Five minutes after the bite, the victim becomes dizzy and short of breath. The bite

*D*espite its pretty appearance, the blue-ringed octopus poses a serious threat to humans.

can cause death within two to three hours. Most disturbing from a medical point of view is the fact that laboratory animals do not form antibodies against the blue-ringed octopus's venom. That makes producing an effective antivenin extremely difficult.

The good news is that these animals are easily avoided. They go out of their way to stay clear of people and are reluctant to bite unless provoked. Most human injuries occur when people find what they think is a cute, pretty little octopus in the water and hold it in their hand to show others.

⤳ *A HOTBED OF POISONOUS ANIMALS* ⤳

Although travel brochures avoid mentioning the fact, many of the deadliest animals in the world live within a few dozen miles of the coast of the world's smallest continent. The most lethal of the cnidaria (the sea wasp), the most poisonous mollusks (blue-ringed octopuses, and cone shells), and the most feared poisonous fish (the stonefish) are all neighbors in the shallow ocean waters near Australia's beaches.

The poison does not stop at the water's edge. Australia is home to more than 50 poisonous snakes, including the land species with the most toxic venom drop for drop (the brown snake), and the snake with the most lethal dose of venom per bite (the taipan). The deadly funnel-web spider also makes its home exclusively in Australia, as does one of the world's few poisonous mammals, the platypus.

Even in Australia, however, encounters with poisonous creatures are so rare that nature lovers can safely enjoy the outdoors by observing common sense and a few precautions.

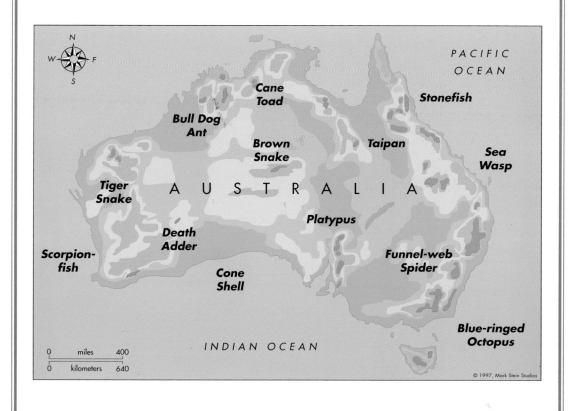

CONE SHELLS   The gracefully patterned scrolls of the cone shells are so intricate and attractive that collectors have actively sought them for centuries. Single specimens of cone shells may sell for thousands of dollars.

However, beautiful colors and patterns in nature often serve as warning signs of danger. Cone shells are no exception. The most stunning shells are often deadly to humans as well as to the small animals on which the cone shells prey.

In this sequence of photographs, a purple cone snail stalks, then catches, and eventually eats a fish.

Cone shells are actually snails that live inside the hard, protective shells that they create. They are generally quite small, from 1 to 4 inches (2.5 to 10 centimeters) long. Most of the more than 500 species of cone shells live in the Indian and Pacific Oceans, although a few have been found in the tropical Atlantic Ocean. At the beginning of the summer, these creatures move off their homes in the coral reefs and into shallow water to lay eggs.

Cone shells appear so harmless and sluggish that it is difficult to imagine them as predators. But they are equipped with a long, flexible, fleshy protrusion called a proboscis, which extends from the bottom of the shell. At the end of this proboscis are hollow teeth. These can be up to a half inch (1.2 centimeters) long and sharp enough to pierce clothing. When a cone shell finds its prey, it shoots out its proboscis and spears the prey with the teeth.

A cone shell is too slow to track down wounded prey, especially if the intended prey is a quick-swimming animal such as a fish. Nor does the cone shell have arms or claws to pin down a thrashing animal. It must rely on a very fast-acting toxin to disable its victims.

The shells shown here belong to a variety of venomous cone shells. It takes an expert to tell the difference between deadly cone shells and those that are harmless.

Cone shells use one of three different types of neurotoxins, depending on the type of animal they hunt. Some species of cone shells eat worms, others eat mollusks, and others eat fish. The toxin of a worm-eating cone shell tends to work only against worms, and so on.

As a result, worm-eating cone shells present little danger to humans. Only a few mollusk-eating cone shells have been known to harm people. But those cone shells that eat fish that, like humans, are vertebrates, are often deadly to humans. The toxin acts much like cobra venom. It blocks the transmission of nerve signals, and can cause severe itching, dizziness, nausea, breathing difficulty, and temporary paralysis. A few species of cone shells can cause death within a few hours. There is no effective treatment for the venom.

Some cone shells prey upon other cone shells. In these cases, the toxin has no effect either on the prey animal or the predator. The predator simply overpowers its prey.

Like the blue-ringed octopus, venomous cone shells pose a threat only to those humans who decide to disturb them and are careless about it. Cone shells should never be picked up bare-handed. Their proboscis can stretch to a surprising length to reach around and pierce the skin of someone who holds them. Because there are so many species of cone shells, only an experienced specialist can tell the deadly ones from the harmless.

THREE

FISH

As discussed in the Introduction, bright colors and unusual designs often serve as warning flags that alert the natural world to the presence of poison. These very features also make fish attractive to aquarium owners. As a result, some of the most poisonous fish in the sea, scorpionfish, swim in small glass tanks in homes throughout the world.

SCORPIONFISH   The scorpionfish include more than 300 species, among them such descriptively named members as lionfish, zebrafish, and turkeyfish. These are small, slow-swimming predators that prowl along the ocean bottoms at a variety of depths. Most live in the Indian and Pacific Oceans and are particularly abundant in the waters near Australia.

Brilliant colors and stripes actually serve opposite purposes in different species of scorpionfish. Some spread their gaudy fins as a warning to predators. In other species, the coloring actually serves as camouflage to disguise the fish as it lurks on the bottom of the sea, waiting for prey to wander within range.

Because they are slow swimmers, scorpionfish rely on stealth to catch most of their meals. They hide in crevices, behind rocks, under debris, or lie motionless on the ocean bottom, camouflaged against their surroundings.

When a small fish or crustacean swims within range, most scorpionfish swallow the prey with their wide mouths in one quick gulp. Turkeyfish are slightly more active. They brush the ocean bottom with their fins to roust small crustaceans. They sometimes work together to surround a school of fish so that none can escape their attack.

Scorpionfish do not inflict poison with their bite. Their toxin lies in dozens of spines that protrude from their fins. Each spine rests loosely in a sheath of skin that contains a venom gland. The spine can penetrate an animal, but the sheath does not. As the spine penetrates, the sheath gets pushed back, squeezing the gland so that the poison flows into the wound.

The scorpionfish's poison does not serve to bring down prey; rather it is a defensive weapon against other predators. Being slow swimmers, scorpionfish do not try to swim away from danger. When threatened, the turkeyfish lowers its head, snaps its jaws, and arches its back to point its poisonous dorsal spines at the attacker. Lionfish open their mouths wide and hold their poisonous spines in a rigid position.

Lionfish use their venom to defend themselves, not to capture prey.

Scorpionfish venom is seldom deadly to humans, but it can cause extreme pain. Anyone who cuts a hand or foot on a scorpionfish spine suffers immediate burning pain. In extreme cases, cardiac arrest and unconsciousness can result. The severity of the injury depends on the number of poisonous spines that puncture the skin.

STONEFISH   Although beautiful designs and vivid colors often indicate poison in nature, there are glaring exceptions. The stonefish is a reddish brown, warty, knobby creature with eyes spaced far apart. It looks like a rotting piece of wood or a chunk of rock covered with patches of moss and

---

~ POISON MYSTERIES ~

In some of nature's deadliest creatures, scientists are unsure of the exact role that poison plays. Stonefish not only contain deadly venom in their spines but also are covered with poisonous skin. Why are these fish practically oozing poison? Even without poison, the fish's lancelike spines could inflict a wound painful enough to discourage most creatures from disturbing it. The stonefish's defenses are so formidable that the creature has virtually no natural enemies. The only evidence of a stonefish being eaten by a predator has been the remains of a single stonefish found in the digestive tract of a seasnake.

Can the stonefish thank its venom for this freedom from predators? Even if venom provides an extra measure of protection, what is the advantage in having such an incredibly deadly venom?

Fish with poisonous organs are a different sort of mystery. How does a fish benefit from poison that does not take effect until after the fish is killed and eaten? If the poison is strong enough to kill the predator, as is the case with many fish, then the predator cannot learn to leave other members of the species alone. In this case, ichthyologists (scientists who study fish) wonder if poison is simply a byproduct of other body processes. They note that fish tend to be most toxic at the peak of their reproductive cycles. Perhaps the poison is a side effect of sexual chemical changes.

Enough such mysteries exist surrounding the presence of venom in fish and in other creatures to keep researchers busy for a long time.

---

fungus. It also happens to be the most poisonous fish in the sea. As with many other highly venomous creatures, stonefish live in the shallow waters off the northeast coast of Australia, as well as near Saudi Arabia.

The stonefish's ugly features serve as a disguise. It seldom swims about. Instead it lies on the ocean floor where it blends with its surroundings. Sometimes it partially buries itself in the sand or mud so that it looks like a stone or some piece of nonliving matter that has fallen into the water. The 12-inch- (5-centimeter-) long stonefish lies perfectly still as smaller fish swim close. Suddenly it sucks its prey into its large, upturned mouth.

As with the scorpionfish, stonefish poison serves for self-defense. The stonefish flares its 13 dorsal spines erect at the slightest threat. These needle-sharp spines are surrounded by fleshy sheaths containing large venom glands. As the spines jab into flesh, the sheaths fall back and the poison flows through two grooves in the spines into the wound.

Stonefish are especially dangerous to humans. They are so well-camouflaged that they are almost impossible to see. Their sharp, sturdy spines can pierce gloves, flippers, and even rubber-soled shoes.

Camouflage makes stonefish virtually impossible to spot, whether in this photograph, or on the ocean floor.

Stonefish venom is so potent that the prick of a single spine can cause a person to shriek and thrash in agony. The wound is pale in the center, surrounded by red swollen tissue. The paralyzing damage can be widespread and long-lasting. One marine researcher stung on the hand was unable to use that hand for almost three months.

If several spines penetrate a foot or hand, the victim may die a painful death within hours unless treated immediately. Even prompt treatment with antivenin is not always successful. The venom maintains its potency so well that even a dead stonefish can inflict an excruciating, disabling injury.

TOADFISH   The toadfish is another poisonous, unsightly, big-mouthed bottom-dweller of the ocean. Toadfish are more common than stonefish. They can be found in both the Atlantic and Pacific Oceans. Their painful stings are not as deadly as those of the stonefish. Toadfish avoid many unnecessary encounters with larger creatures by scaring them off with a loud grunt.

CATFISH   The bewhiskered catfish is far more familiar to most people than the scorpionfish. The catfish's facial projections, known as barbels, are not poisonous. But these long, scaleless fish produce venom near small, barbed spines in front of their dorsal fins and in their pectoral fins. These spines can be locked in a rigid position to protect the catfish from predators.

There are more than 2,400 species of catfish. North American catfish, a

---

～ KIDDIE POISON ～

Because adults are capable of producing much more toxin than youngsters of the same species, they are usually far more poisonous. The situation, however, is reversed in the case of the common aquarium fish known as scats. These fish are generally scavengers, feeding off dead organisms in the Indian and Pacific Oceans.

Juvenile scats have strong spines with which they can inflict a toxin. In humans, the effect is mild pain and swelling. As the fish grows, however, its poison glands shrink. Although the adult retains the strong spines, it completely loses its ability to produce venom.

common item on many restaurant menus, are not dangerous. But a large commercial South American catfish can cause painful and deadly wounds. Two species of the Asian catfish that swim in waters from India to Vietnam are even more dangerous. Although most catfish sting only when handled, the Asian catfish will actually attack when threatened.

STINGRAYS   Rays are large, flattened fish that swim in a motion similar to that of birds or bats flying through the air. Their horizontal shape enables them bury themselves in the sand and to root out clams and other invertebrates from the ocean bottom. Not all rays are poisonous, but stingrays definitely are. Their tails end in a barbed spine covered with a thin layer of skin. That skin peels away when the ray's spine enters flesh, exposing the barbs. Venom produced in tissue in the grooves of the spine enter the wound. The venom causes a painful, swollen wound that heals slowly.

As with most fish, the stingray uses its poison purely for defense.

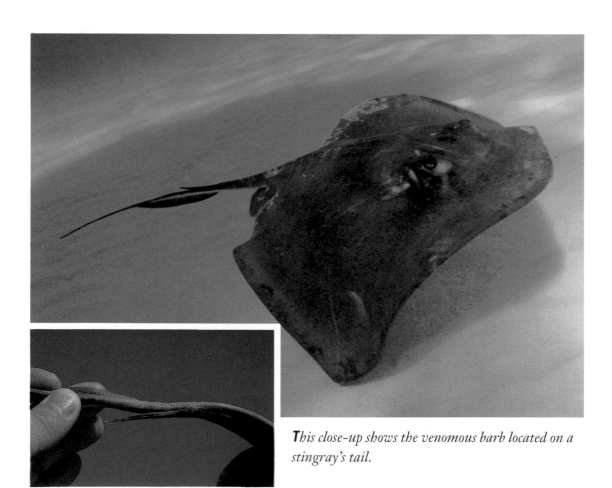

This close-up shows the venomous barb located on a stingray's tail.

PUFFERS   Puffers, also called blowfish or fugu, store one of the most deadly poisons known to the animal kingdom. No animal, however, has anything to fear from a live puffer because the fish has no way of injecting that poison into another creature.

More than 100 species of puffers live in the ocean, primarily off the coasts of Japan, Korea, India, and the South Pacific. Puffers are large fish that can grow up to 3 feet (1 meter) long and weigh up to 30 pounds (14 kilograms). They get their name from the fact that they can puff up to double their size when threatened. They do this by sucking air or water into an internal sac.

The poison found in the fish's intestines, ovaries, and especially in the liver is 25 times more powerful than the poison of the deadly poison dart

Japanese people consider pufffers to be a delicacy. Puffers are safe when prepared properly, but puffer poisoning is a real risk.

frog. It is 275 times more deadly than cyanide. A single milligram of this substance, an amount that would fit on the head of a pin, can easily kill a human. No one knows exactly why the puffer's organs are so full of poison. It may be a byproduct of the production of poison in the fish's skin that is highly effective at repelling potential predators.

Back in the 1700s, famed British explorer Captain James Cook and his crew made the mistake of taking nibbles of puffer meat. Cook reported, "We were seized with extraordinary weakness." They were fortunate that they took small bites.

The toxicity of the puffer would seem to be a good reason to avoid eating such a fish at all. But the Japanese consider the puffer, when stripped of its poisonous organs, to be one of the most delicious treats from the sea. They eat so many of these fish that they have reduced the puffer population's numbers to alarmingly low levels. More than 20 Japanese die of puffer poisoning each year, usually from fish inexpertly cleaned at home.

FOUR

SPIDERS, SCORPIONS, AND CENTIPEDES

*T*he idea of being surrounded by millions of poisonous animals strikes many people as one of the most frightening of nightmares. But this is not merely a fantastic script for a horror movie—this is reality. Many people are never more than a few feet away from a poisonous creature and they are often within shouting distance of thousands. A field researcher calculated that a single acre of New England pasture harbors more than two million spiders.

SPIDERS   Virtually all of the 50,000 species of spiders are poisonous. In most cases, though, spider venom poses no threat to anything larger than an insect or another spider. A few of the largest species occasionally catch and kill small lizards and even birds. But most spider venom has no effect at all on larger animals, with the exception of monkeys and humans. Spiders generally have fangs that are too small to break through human skin. Even those that can bite people are usually too small to produce enough poison to cause more than the mildest of irritations.

Spiders are small predators whose eight legs often make them seem larger than they are. They use a neurotoxin to disable or kill their prey. Spiders inject this poison through curved fangs connected to poison glands in or at the base of the mouth. By contracting the muscles surrounding these glands, the spider can regulate the amount of venom it puts into a bite.

Spiders are not able to break down or chew their prey into pieces small enough to swallow. They digest prey outside their bodies by pumping it full of digestive juices. Then they suck up the resulting fluids, leaving the undigested insect shell behind.

Only a few spiders are the large, aggressive hunters depicted in horror movies. The African baboon spider is a long-legged spider that raises its front legs when disturbed and may even attack when it feels threatened. Its bite is similar to a bee sting to humans.

South American huntsman spiders may have a body as big as 1½ inches (4 centimeters) in diameter, plus large, hairy legs. The bird-eating spider is even larger measuring 10 inches (25 centimeters) in diameter, including its legs. This nocturnal spider also acts aggressively. Its bite causes humans severe pain and cramps, and has been known to result in death within five hours. The spider is common enough in Brazil that the country has a large supply of antivenin for its bite, ready to be rushed to the aid of a victim.

The South American huntsman spider agressively hunts its prey.

Funnel-web Spider   Perhaps the deadliest spider in the world is the funnel-web spider of Australia. This spider has a brown abdomen that can grow to the size of a cherry, and a black thorax. It has a coffin-shaped head, a light-colored throat, and orange eyes. Its fangs are ⅓ inch (one centimeter) long and tough enough to bite through a child's fingernail or a beetle's shell.

Like most spiders, funnel-web spiders hide in dark corners and holes, primarily in rock crevices and house foundations. The spider gets its common name from the tube of dense webbing it weaves to funnel prey into its lair. The funnel-web spider is aggressive and may rear up on its hind legs to bite. Unlike many of the deadliest spiders, the male is the more poisonous sex.

The venom of the funnel-web spider causes an overload of nervous impulses to the muscles and organs of its prey. The acid in the venom immediately begins to break down the prey into a nutritious soup. A human victim of a funnel-web spider bite experiences twitching, excessive sweating, and salivating. The venom is potent enough to kill a child within an hour, an adult within a few days.

**R**esidents of Sydney, Australia, need to be able to recognize a funnel-web spider when they see one.

Sydney funnel-web spiders are particularly dangerous because they live in the highly populated urban area of Sydney, Australia. This gives them frequent contact with humans. Antivenin for funnel-web spider bites did not exist for many years because laboratory animals injected with the toxin did not produce antibodies against it. Finally, in 1980, Australian researcher Struan Sutherland succeeded in developing an antivenin that dramatically saved the life of a 49-year-old man the first time it was tried.

Black Widow

Large, hairy, aggressive spiders are generally dangerous only to their prey. The spiders most toxic to humans tend to be small and rather plain-looking. The best-known of the small, lethal spiders is the black widow. This spider gets its name from the tendency of the females to kill the much smaller males and from the fact that only the females bite.

Black widows are only about ½ to ¾ inch (1.3 to 2 centimeters) in diameter. They have round, bulbous, shiny black abdomens with a distinctive red or orange double triangle on their undersides that resembles an hourglass.

Black widows can be found in most of the world, including most of the mainland United States. People hardly ever see them, however, because they are extremely shy. They build their irregular webs in dark, secluded areas in the corners of houses, sheds, barns, and other buildings.

The black widow hangs upside down at the edge of the web and awaits the arrival of its prey. Because it is nearly blind, the black widow relies on the vibrations of the trapped prey to direct it. As soon as the black widow senses prey on the web, it dashes out and injects the prey with its venom. Then the spider wraps the prey in silk and waits for the venom to digest it.

Only female black widow spiders show the distinctive red or orange hourglass markings.

Black widows are not aggressive and seldom bite people even when provoked. When threatened, they retreat to a corner of the web and freeze, hoping to be left alone. Most black widow bites of humans occur when the spider is crushed by someone who does not see it. In the past, this often happened in outhouses, a common home of the black widow, where the spider was trapped in the seat and had no alternative but to bite.

For years, some experts scoffed at claims that the black widow was dangerous. But in the late 1930s, medical professionals confirmed fatalities from black widow bites. The neurotoxin of the black widow, in fact, blocks nerve signals more effectively than that of rattlesnakes. A victim of a black widow bite feels no discomfort from the initial bite. But 10 to 60 hours later, intense pain arises at the spot of the bite and spreads. Muscles become rigid. The victim suffers from nausea, headaches, excessive sweating, labored breathing, even shock. Most recover completely within two to three days, especially if they receive antivenin treatment. But about 1 in 20 untreated cases results in death, usually from lung paralysis. One or two people die each year in the United States from black widow bites.

Brown Recluse   Another unpretentious spider with lethal potential is the brown recluse or fiddleback. These small, long-legged spiders prefer to hide in dry, dark corners. They can be found in the crevices of basements, attics, and sheds, in bookshelves, and under objects and litter. They exist throughout the United States and into Central America, although they are more common in the southwestern United States.

Like black widows, brown recluses are shy and unaggressive. They bite only when caught between bare flesh and some other object. Because brown recluses hunt at night, they are less likely than black widows to come in contact with humans.

Only in recent years have people discovered the toxicity of these spiders. Their bite causes a slight sting at first. Within two to eight hours the pain increases. The bite reddens and then forms a purple, star-shaped wound. The venom actually destroys muscle and fat. In some cases, doctors must remove the affected tissue. In other cases, the wound forms a large, crusty, red scar.

When the venom penetrates into the internal organs, death results about 30 percent of the time, within one to three days. Otherwise, 94 percent of victims recover even without treatment.

*N*ot *particularly threatening in appearance, the brown recluse spider can be toxic.*

CENTIPEDES   Most of the flattened, long-bodied, insectlike creatures known as centipedes are not at all dangerous. But there are centipedes, primarily in the tropics, that can inflict venomous damage. The most poisonous ones are large centipedes up to 13 inches (33 centimeters) long, containing about 20 segments and two to three dozen pairs of legs.

These centipedes live in damp places under stones and rotting logs and feed on slow-moving insects and worms. They have a pair of hooklike appendages called maxillipeds under the head for catching and holding their prey. These maxillipeds are connected by ducts to a venom gland so that centipedes can inject their poison while clutching their prey.

SCORPIONS   Scorpions are a class of spiderlike creatures that carry an even more fearsome reputation than spiders. Mexicans alone suffer an estimated 70,000 scorpion stings per year, with more than 1,000 of them fatal.

The scorpions include at least 1,500 species that thrive in all types of habitats. Although they are most commonly associated with the deserts of southwestern North America, northern Africa, the Middle East, and tropical rain forests, they can also be found in grasslands and in mountains. Blind, pale scorpions have even been discovered in deep caves beyond the reach of sunlight. All scorpions are poisonous.

Scorpions have a unique system of delivering their venom. Unlike spiders, who use their mouths, scorpions strike with stingers at the tips of their tails. Near the stinger is a bulb called a telson that contains two venom glands. The tail arches high over the scorpion's back as the animal moves in for a strike. A scorpion can whip its stinger forward with lightning speed.

Combined with the pair of pincers or pedipalps outstretched at the front, the scorpion appears heavily armed. Actually, the pedipalps are usually of more use than the stinger in capturing prey. The stinger is more often used as a defensive weapon than for securing food.

Scorpions spend the daylight hours hiding in cool, dark, dry places. They do most of their hunting at dusk or at night. Spiders, insects, and other scorpions make up most scorpions' meals. Some of the largest species may kill an occasional frog or small rodent. They locate their prey with their sense of hearing. Like spiders they digest their prey with acids and enzymes before eating it.

Female scorpions have a long life span for such small creatures, from 15 to 25 years. They do not usually mate until they are seven years old. After a pregnancy that can usually last several months, they give live birth to babies that are fully formed miniature versions of adults.

Scorpions are poisonous from the moment they are born. Their toxin affects the nervous system, often paralyzing the prey. Almost all scorpion stings are painful, but only about 25 species are dangerous to humans. Even the deadliest of scorpions do not usually kill adults. Generally speaking, the

---

∾ FATAL ATTRACTION ∾

For both spiders and scorpions, mating can be a perilous time for the male. The male is usually smaller than the female, sometimes less than half its size. Occasionally, the female turns its venom on its smaller mate. About 10 percent of the females eat the males after mating.

The only dangerous scorpion found in the United States is the bark scorpion. Its young are poisonous at birth.

paler the color and the smaller the pedipalps, the more venomous the scorpion.

Scorpion Attacks

Unfortunately, many of the most highly toxic scorpions tend to live near populated areas. After a night of hunting, many scorpions seek refuge in shoes, clothes, and bedsheets. Bites most frequently occur when people put on shoes or clothes without checking, or roll over on a scorpion.

One type of scorpion, which lives in and around houses in eastern Brazil, kills more than 100 people per year, mostly children. About 5 to 10 percent of small children stung by these scorpions die from respiratory and cardiac failure. These scorpions apparently reproduce asexually, because no males have ever been found.

The slender, 4-inch (10-centimeter) Sahara scorpion that ranges from North Africa to India may have the deadliest sting. One out of every five stings results in death.

The only dangerous scorpion in the United States is the bark scorpion, also called the sculptured scorpion, which lives in Arizona. Unfortunately, this dangerous creature is almost impossible to distinguish from many relatively harmless species of scorpions.

The scorpions' stingers do not protect them from all predators. Owls, bats, and snakes regularly eat scorpions.

FIVE

INSECTS

At least two-thirds of all identified species of animals belong to the insect family—more than a million species. Insects do not have the reputation of spiders and scorpions for wielding poison. Most insects are so small that we do not even think of them when we put together lists of the world's deadliest creatures. Yet in many parts of the world, the most lethal venomous animal you are likely to encounter is an insect.

HONEYBEE   In the United States and other cool weather countries, the deadliest animal of all is the familiar honeybee. Honeybees account for one-fourth of all deaths by animal poisoning in the United States each year. They kill nearly as many people as all venomous snakes combined.

The honeybee was originally a native of Europe and Asia. It was domesticated because of its ability to produce sweet honey and brought over to the Western Hemisphere.

Honeybees live on plant matter rather than meat. Therefore, they have no use for poison as a means of getting food, and they use it only in defense. The rear of a honeybee holds a single barbed stinger. The stinger does not really defend the bee from danger because it dies almost immediately after using it. The barb of the stinger hooks so firmly into the object of its attack that the bee cannot safely pull it out. When it tries, a large part of the bee's body, including vital organs, stays behind with the stinger in the flesh of the victim. Also left behind with the stinger are the venom glands, which may continue to release venom for several minutes after the bee has broken away.

Obviously, the venom does not help the individual honeybee to survive. But the bee is a social animal, and the venom serves to protect the bee colony. The sterile worker bees (females who are unable to reproduce), who make up most of the population of a hive, respond to threats not only to themselves but also to other members of the hive. When any bee is threatened, it releases a chemical. This signals other bees in the area that danger is at hand, and they rush to the defense of the threatened bee.

Honeybees rarely sting unless disturbed, usually by frightened people who instinctively swat at them. When they do sting, their venom is not particularly toxic. It usually produces only minor, temporary pain and swelling. The danger lies in allergic reactions to the venom. Those who are allergic to bee venom may experience anaphylactic shock—a failure of the circulatory system. Symptoms of anaphylactic shock include rashes, severe swelling, and difficulty breathing. Some victims who are allergic to bee venom have died within minutes from a single sting. Contrary to what occurs with most animal venom, adults tend to react more violently than children to bee stings. Those who react severely to bee stings often own an injection kit that includes a substance that counteracts the effects of anaphylactic shock. If an allergic person is stung, an immediate injection may save his or her life.

Killer Bees: Threat or Overblown Scare?

During the 1950s, beekeepers in Brazil imported a subspecies of honeybee from Africa. These bees tend to produce more honey than other honeybees in warm-weather climates. They also happen to be more aggressive and protective of their hives than other honeybees. A single threatened African bee gives off an odor that may bring hundreds of bees to the attack. African bees are not content with merely driving off invaders but may chase and sting them more than a half mile (800 meters) from the hive. The overwhelming number of stings from an angry mass of African bees may introduce a dangerous amount of venom into the victim.

Some of the African bees brought to São Paulo, Brazil, escaped into the wild. They began killing less aggressive bees and taking over their territory. Reports of African bee swarms killing people, horses, and cattle hit the press, which dubbed these insects "killer bees." By 1975 the bees had spread over much of South America and began expanding their territory northward. Seven years later they were moving through Panama.

The press warned that killer bees were on their way to the United States and could create a serious danger to Americans. The motion picture industry capitalized on people's fear of the deadly bees, producing several movies with killer bee disaster plots. In 1990 the United States Department of Agriculture located a swarm of killer bees in Texas. They immediately destroyed the bees.

Scientists say that the danger presented by African bees, who as yet have barely penetrated the borders of Texas, New Mexico, and Arizona, has

Despite the frenzy stirred up by the media, it is possible to work with African killer bees safely.

been greatly exaggerated. The African bee toxin is no more dangerous than that of the European honeybee, and attacks are not as common as sometimes reported. Fewer than eight deaths per year have been attributed to killer bee attacks since the 1950s in Brazil. When left alone, the African bees intermingle with other honeybees, a circumstance that tends to dilute their aggressiveness.

BUMBLEBEES   Bumblebees appear to be more dangerous than honeybees simply because of their larger size. But even though they can sting repeatedly and cause painful welts, bumblebees rarely sting unless greatly provoked. They seldom produce the allergic reactions that make honeybee stings so potentially dangerous.

WASPS   The family of stinging insects known as wasps are similar to bees in appearance. They can be distinguished by their longer, more slender bodies. Wasps build nests in trees, in the ground, and under the eaves of buildings. A tropical wasp constructs cone-shaped nests over 3 feet (1 meter) in diameter. These nests, which hang from trees, may each house more than 1,000 wasps.

Wasps are usually reluctant to sting. But, unlike honeybees, they can sting repeatedly without killing themselves. A large group of wasps can inflict painful damage on anything that disturbs their nest.

Some wasps use their toxin for preying on insects and spiders rather than strictly for defense.

⁓ POISON AGAINST POISON ⁓

The tarantula wasp lives dangerously. It is a predator that specializes in killing not helpless insects but tarantulas. Occasionally a wasp will lose a battle with a tarantula. But most of the time, it succeeds in paralyzing the spider with its sting. The wasp then drags the tarantula to a burrow it has dug in the sand, lays an egg on the spider, and seals the burrow. When the wasp larva hatches from the egg, it feeds on the still-living, immobile tarantula.

A tarantula wasp confronts prey that is much larger than itself. It thrusts its abdomen toward the tarantula, in preparation for attack. Finally, the wasp stings the spider, paralyzing it with its venom.

ANTS   Ants are among the most common insects, and the vast majority of the eight to ten thousand species are quite harmless. But ants do have a stinging apparatus with which they can inject a mild solution of chemicals. Some use their stingers primarily in defense of their colony, while others use them to kill the insects they eat.

In certain species, this sting can be severe enough to cause itching, burning, and even more serious complications in their human victims. Fireants congregate by the thousands in nests up to 3 feet (1 meter) in diameter. They can form hundreds of these mounds per acre, ruining farm fields. Each fireant can sting repeatedly, leaving a small blister each time. Multiple stings from a large colony, especially when combined with an allergic reaction can cause breathing difficulties and even, in rare cases, death.

Ever since fireants arrived in the United States in the 1930s (probably aboard a ship from South America), they have caused increasing problems. Roughly 75,000 people, most of them in the Southeast, receive treatment each year for stings from fireants. Americans have tried unsuccessfully to use poisons of their own to kill off the ants. Recently, researchers have

Fireants can be a serious nuisance. Here, workers apply pesticide to a cluster of fireant nests.

found a new weapon with which to fight fireants—a parasitic fly that lays eggs only in fireant bodies. The maggots (fly larvae) eat their way up to the ants' heads, killing them.

Australian bulldog ants may be the most dangerous ants of all. These ants, which grow as large as an inch (2.5 centimeters) long, produce a more powerful venom than other ants and in far greater quantities. They live in large colonies and react violently to any threat.

CATERPILLARS   Many caterpillars are protected by poisonous chemicals that discourage predators from eating them. The fat, juicy io moth caterpillar, for example, is a tempting target for birds and other predators. This caterpillar, common in the southeastern United States, is covered with tufts of hair in which several sharp spines are embedded. The spines are connected to venom glands that produce a burning, foul-tasting substance.

The saddleback caterpillar has long spines at both ends of its body as well as smaller ones along its sides. The toxin produced by larvae of this species can produce severe, long-lasting pain, swelling, and nausea in humans.

Although it may look soft and fuzzy, it's definitely best not to pick up a flannel moth caterpillar.

49

Perhaps the most toxic caterpillar is that of the small, brown flannel moth. This caterpillar bristles with a dense covering of stinging hairs. Contact with the flannel moth caterpillar can produce a severe rash and leave a red blister that lingers for a week.

In most cases the caterpillar's poison defense does not protect it from harm. They benefit by predators learning from the miserable experience and leaving other members of the species alone in the future.

BUTTERFLIES   Butterflies belong to a group of insects with short life spans. Few adult butterflies live much longer than a week or two. Passion vine butterflies, however, can live up to twenty-five times longer than the average butterfly.

One advantage they have going for them is that they are, in the words of one expert, "flying cyanide capsules." They are able to synthesize the deadly poison cyanide from the nectar or pollen of one of their favorite plants, the passion vine.

Passion vine butterflies create cyanide within their bodies in order to defend themselves from predators.

The cyanide does not affect the butterflies. But it makes them taste bad to birds, who quickly learn to recognize their brilliant markings and leave them alone. Several nonpoisonous butterfly species with similar markings benefit when predators mistake them for passion vine butterflies.

Passion vine butterflies do not fit the usual image of the gentle, flighty butterfly. Because their poison renders them off-limits to predators, passion vine butterflies can get away with being rather slow, unelusive fliers. Many passion vine caterpillars eat members of their own species. They mate so aggressively that they have been known to punch holes in chrysalides to get at and mate with pupae. Their relatively long lives give them time to develop sharp memories and other higher functions of the brain not seen in other butterflies.

SNAKES

When people think of venom, the image that comes to mind most often is a hissing, coiling snake. Snakes are the largest venomous predators on earth. Of the more than 2,500 species of snakes, about 650 use venom to bring down their prey.

Poisonous snakes are found throughout the world with the exception of islands such as Ireland and New Zealand and extremely cold lands. Because they rely on external heat to warm their bodies, snakes do not do well in cold weather climates. A venomous snake is probably too sluggish to strike at a temperature below 50 degrees Fahrenheit (10 degrees Celsius).

Snakes are remarkable hunters, given their limitations. They do not see well but they make good use of other senses. A snake takes tiny air samples with its tongue and presents them to the Jacobson's organ in the roof of its mouth. By analyzing the chemicals in these samples, the Jacobson's organ alerts the snake to the presence of prey, predators, or mates. Snakes can also sense vibrations and body heat. All of this helps a snake to locate its prey.

FANGS   Poisonous snakes inject their poison through a pair of long, hollow or grooved teeth known as fangs. Fangs are connected by ducts to reservoirs of poison located in the snake's cheek. These bulging sacs often give the snake's head the swollen, triangular shape that distinguishes many poisonous snakes from nonvenomous ones.

A snake's strike is an intricately timed, astonishingly well-coordinated event. In a lightning fast motion, it can propel its body toward its prey with deadly accuracy. One researcher trying to feed a mouse to an Australian brown snake lost his grip on the mouse. The rodent dashed up the researcher's arm. The snake uncoiled a perfect strike that reached out of its cage and picked the sprinting mouse off the man's arm without touching his skin. At the instant that a viper unleashes its furious strike, it rotates its jaw. This allows the large fangs, which are folded back against the roof of the mouth, to come forward into biting position. The snake bites the prey, squeezes its poison sacs to inject the poison, and returns to its original position. All of this happens too quickly for the human eye to see.

Fangs are rather fragile and frequently break off. Venomous snakes have extra fangs at the sides of their faces to replace those that break.

MEASURING THE DOSE
Venomous snakes do not automatically release a set amount of poison every time they strike. Their venom sacs are surrounded by muscles that give the snakes control over the amount of poison injected.

Venom is a precious commodity, and snakes do not waste it. They may not bother to inject poison into small, harmless prey. The Australian tiger snake needs little if any poison to subdue frogs. It swallows the amphibians immediately after biting them. The same snake, however, cannot catch and consume a living, clawed rodent without a fight that may cause harm to itself. In these situations, it injects its poison and retreats out of harm's way until the poison takes effect. When the rodent is dead or paralyzed, the snake returns to eat its meal.

Snakes do not necessarily use their venom when biting in self-defense, either. Snakes prefer to avoid battles with larger, stronger animals that they cannot eat. First, they try to warn away the animal with noises or with a menacing show, such as the spreading hood of the cobra. If that does not work, they may try to scare off the animal by striking. Because they do not intend to kill the animal, they often decline to waste poison on these bites. A British research team found that 30 to 50 percent of bites from terrestrial venomous snakes, and 80 percent of sea snake bites are poison-free or "dry" bites. This characteristic of controlling the amount of poison injected often confuses people as to whether a certain species is dangerous or not.

POISON SALIVA   Snake venom is a highly evolved form of saliva that contains various proteins. The group of snakes known as elapids generally produce neurotoxins that interfere with nerve messages that regulate the heart and lungs. Vipers rely on hemotoxin that causes tissue damage and affects the blood. A few snakes such as mambas and certain rattlesnakes may have some of both. The exact form of toxin varies from species to species and even between members of the same species.

Snakes and spiders have a similar problem in that they have no means of breaking down their prey into easily swallowed pieces. While spiders compensate by digesting their prey before eating it, snakes swallow their prey whole. The two halves of a snake's lower jaw are connected only by muscle and ligament, not by bone. This, plus its elastic skin, allows a snake to swallow prey larger than its entire head. If humans had the same elastic jaw structure as a snake, we could swallow a watermelon whole.

The deadliest snakes in the world are those with poison fangs located at

A *western diamondback rattlesnake has no trouble swallowing a wood rat whole.*

the front of the mouth. Herpetologists (scientists who study snakes) divide these front-fanged snakes into elapids and vipers.

ELAPIDS   Elapids have short, immovable fangs that are always in position to bite. They are most commonly found in the Eastern Hemisphere. Elapids include sea snakes, cobras, mambas, kraits, coral snakes, and more than seventy species of poisonous Australian serpents.

Sea Snakes   Almost all of the more than 50 species of sea snakes are highly poisonous. Sea snakes are closely related to cobras, but have special adaptations for living in water. They can absorb enough oxygen through their skin to stay under water for up to two hours while active and for much longer periods while at rest. Their tails are broadened and flattened to propel them through the water. This adaptation makes most sea snakes virtually helpless on land.

Sea snakes generally grow to about 3 to 4 feet (3 to 3.2 meters), although some species may exceed 8 feet (3.5 meters). They live primarily in the tropical waters of the Pacific Ocean, especially in shallow waters around reefs and river mouths where the currents and waves are less severe than in the open sea. They may congregate by the hundreds of thousands during mating season.

Sea snakes primarily prey upon eels and other long fish. They can locate prey even in muddy waters through the detection of vibrations and biochemicals. Their senses are so highly developed that the snakes can determine the location and speed of the prey and therefore can make accurate strikes. They can also determine the size of nearby creatures and not waste an attack on anything too large for them. A seaman swimming in the Pacific Ocean near Panama suddenly found himself in what many would consider their worst nightmare—surrounded by thousands of writhing sea snakes. None of the snakes, however, bothered him in the least. Even when these mild-mannered snakes do bite people, they usually inject little or no venom.

Sea snakes are not particularly agile or fast swimmers. They either lurk in crevices to ambush their unsuspecting prey or trap their prey in a small area, such as against a reef. Their neurotoxin is the most lethal of all snake venoms, and attacks muscle tissues. The toxin allows the sea snake to strike quickly against dangerous prey, such as moray eels, and then dart out of harm's way while the poison does its work.

Cobras   Cobras are among the most easily recognized snakes, at least when they are riled. At such times, they raise their heads high off the ground and spread their special ribs into a distinctive, wide hood.

Cobras live in Asia and Africa. Many species thrive near populated areas that do not have hospital facilities where snakebites can be treated. About 20 percent of untreated cobra bites result in death. Cobra venom, like that of most elapids, is neurotoxic. Effects in humans include pain, swelling, dizziness, weak pulse, convulsions, shock, and paralysis.

The king cobra is easily the largest poisonous animal in the world. These snakes can grow nearly 18 feet (5.5 meters) long. They can raise their speed up the process. The less the limbs move, the more slowly the poison will spread through the body.

4) Keep the victim as calm as possible. Fear and panic can increase the speed of the absorption of poison. Also, some people are so frightened of snakes that a snakebite can send them into shock or even cause a heart attack.

5) Evacuate the victim to a medical facility.

6) Observe the symptoms. The severity of the symptoms and the quickness with which the venom takes effect indicate how much venom is in the system. This information helps physicians determine the correct dosage of antivenin. Venomous snakes do not always inject poison into their bites. If no symptoms appear, treatment may not be necessary.

All venomous snakes should be avoided or approached with caution. However, people should not fear going out in nature because of snakes. Snakes are rarely aggressive toward anything as large as a human and will not strike unless provoked or cornered. About 80 percent of snakebites occur when people try to catch or kill snakes.

Most snakebites can be prevented by wearing boots and long pants and looking where you put your hands. With prompt medical treatment, most people survive the bites of even the most poisonous snakes.

heads 4 feet (1.2 meters) off the ground and can inject more venom than any other snake, over two teaspoonsful. When they strike, king cobras hang onto their prey (primarily snakes) and chew the poison into the wound.

Fortunately, king cobras tend to avoid human habitations more than most cobras, and usually retreat when they encounter people. King cobras are one of the few kinds of snakes that build a nest for their eggs and curl themselves around the eggs to protect them.

Spitting cobras live in Central Africa and Asia. Their fangs have openings near the tips, which allows them to shoot a dilute form of venom at an intended target. These snakes aim for the eyes of their prey, which they can

A *spectacled cobra is an impressive sight, both front and back, when it spreads its hood.*

hit accurately from a distance of 7 feet (2.1 meters). The venom produces temporary, painful blindness in the victim.

Taipans   Perhaps the most feared snake in the world is the taipan of the wet forests and dry savannahs of northeastern Australia and New Guinea. This plain brownish snake can grow to more than 12 feet (3.7 meters) in length. Taipans feed exclusively on mammals, which are relatively scarce in Australia, and occasionally on birds. Like all snakes, the taipan is an ectotherm, which means it depends on the environment to regulate its body temperature. Ectotherms (sometimes called cold-blooded animals) require far less energy than endotherms (warm-blooded animals), so a taipan needs to eat only one or two meals per month.

The taipan's search for rats and mice occasionally brings it into contact with humans. The snake retreats from humans unless it feels threatened. Then it turns ferocious. A taipan can strike a half dozen times before a victim has time to react. Its half-inch (1.3-centimeter) long fangs can inject one of the most toxic snake venoms in existence. One bite contains enough venom to kill more than 100,000 mice, or 30 humans. Scientists are baffled as to why the taipan produces such potent venom. The bite of the taipan was almost always fatal until the development of antivenin in 1955.

Mambas   Africans who live in the open savannah south of the Sahara Desert have a great deal of respect for mambas. These thin-bodied snakes, which can grow up to 14 feet (4.3 meters) long, come in both black and bright green species.

Green mambas are agile snakes that often climb trees and bushes in search of prey. Black mambas can slither along the ground with surprising speed. They have been clocked at 8 miles (13 kilometers) per hour, a brisk jogging speed for humans.

A green mamba can be a startling sight perched high in a tree, seeking its prey.

Debates have long raged over which snake holds the dubious honor of being the world's deadliest serpent. Various snakes have a claim on the title, depending on the criteria one uses for determining the most deadly. Sea snakes could be considered the most deadly because they have the most toxic venom, but most experts rate them low on the danger chart because they almost never use their poison against humans.

There is no question that the taipan has the most potent bite. This feature, together with its large size and aggressive nature makes it one of the world's most feared snakes. Black mambas inject a combination of neurotoxin and hemotoxin that makes their bites perhaps the most difficult to treat. The mambas' tendencies to climb trees and to also lift the front half of its body off the ground when striking puts them at a level to inflict injuries to more vulnerable parts of the body.

The enormous king cobra can inject the most poison per bite, up to 500 milligrams. Bushmasters of Central America and puff adders of Africa have long fangs—up to 2 inches (5 centimeters) that can inflict poison deep into their victims, even through protective clothing.

Yet none of these considerations are the key factors in determining which snake causes the most human misery. Venomous snakes that thrive in places with dense human populations, where people go barefoot and bare-legged throughout the year, and where medical facilities are scarce pose a greater threat than larger, more lethal snakes which seldom encounter people.

By some estimates, the Russell's viper ranks as the deadliest snake on earth.

Black mambas are one of the few snakes that may attack without provocation and they can strike with lightning rapidity. They have long, curved fangs capable of delivering a deadly poison that attacks both nerve and muscle fibers. The venom not only works quickly enough to sometimes kill a person within minutes, but also the mixture of both neurotoxin and hemotoxin is difficult to treat with antivenin.

Death Adders Australia's death adder is a short, thick snake, no more than 3 feet (1 meter) long. Its mottled markings blend in so well with

This extremely heavy-bodied snake grows to more than 5 feet (1.5 meters) in length and is distinguished by a series of oval markings that run down its back. The Russell's viper injects a large amount of powerful venom that causes blot clotting.

This viper lives in heavily populated areas of India and Southeast Asia. Although it avoids people, it does not back down when challenged, and will bite repeatedly when cornered. Unlike many snakes that do not like to expose themselves in flat, open ground, the Russell's viper prefers to travel on paths. It often enters houses in search of the mammals, lizards, scorpions, and centipedes that make up its diet. These habits guarantee contact with humans. Because of inadequate medical facilities in areas where the snake lives, Russell's vipers kill an estimated 20,000 people per year.

Many experts rank the saw-scaled viper as even more dangerous than the Russell's viper. This small snake lives in highly populated regions from Nigeria to Sri Lanka. It is so abundant that bounty hunters in the late 19th century collected over 115,000 of them in eight days near Bombay, India. These snakes are frighteningly aggressive—one herpetologist reported that a saw-scaled viper chased him for 40 feet (12 meters) and then struck at his boot. The saw-scaled viper's poison is extremely toxic and hard to treat even when medical facilities are readily available, which is seldom the case in its range.

The World Health Organization estimates that 40,000 people die each year from snakebite, nearly half of them in India. Between them, the saw-scaled viper and Russell's viper probably kill as many people as all other species of snake combined.

the ground that when it lies still, the death adder is almost invisible. While it lies concealed, the snake sometimes waves its brightly colored tail to attract the reptiles and mammals on which it feeds. Its venom serves to digest tissues as well as kill.

Fortunately, death adders do not strike unless extremely provoked. A pair of sugarcane cutters in Australia walked up and down a path all day and never noticed a death adder lying in the middle of it until the sun was almost down. Although their footprints showed they had frequently come within an inch (2.5 centimeters) of stepping on the snake's head, it never struck.

Kraits   Some of the most common and popular snakes of southeast Asia are the kraits. There are a dozen species of these flat-headed elapids, which are related to the cobras. Most reach a maximum length of 3 to 5 feet (1 to 1.5 meters), some grow to as much as 7 feet (2.1 meters). Kraits often live near villages where they eat other snakes, as well as pests such as mice and rats. They also prey upon mammals, lizards, and even fish in rice fields and waterways nearby.

Kraits hunt at night. They are extremely sluggish during the day and are easily captured. They are gentle animals that seldom bite even when provoked, which makes them a favorite among snake dealers. Some krait species so seldom bite that many people who live around them are convinced they are not poisonous.

In fact, one species of krait has a neurotoxin more than 20 times as lethal as that of the king cobra. Kraits have strong jaws that enable them to hold onto their prey and chew in the poison. On the rare occasions when they strike humans, their bite is painless and produces no immediate symptoms for three to five hours. Victims may not even realize they have been bitten until an onslaught of severe symptoms. Once symptoms appear, it is too late to prevent death.

Coral Snakes   The main venomous group of elapids in the Western Hemisphere are the coral snakes. All are colored with some combination of red, black, and yellow bands. This color pattern, however, does not necessarily indicate a coral snake. Snake experts have come up with a number of rhymes concerning coral snake patterns to help distinguish venomous coral snakes from nonvenomous imitators, including:

Red touch yellow, bad for fellow

Red touch black, good for Jack

Coral snakes are small, usually under 3 feet (1 meter) long. They can be found in the United States in forests along the Atlantic coast and in the Southwest. They are nocturnal snakes that hunt lizards and other snakes.

Although many coral snakes have deadly neurotoxin, they seldom cause injuries to humans. They are docile and rarely inject venom even when they do strike. Furthermore, their mouths and fangs are too small to inflict a bite, except on a finger. Even the most deadly Brazilian species of coral

This eastern coral snake with red segments bordered by yellow stripes is poisonous.

snakes have been linked with fewer than one death per year, primarily small children who pick them up, attracted by their bright colors.

VIPERS   Vipers differ from elapids in that they have long, curved, hollow fangs that fold back when not in use. These fangs usually rest against the roof of their mouths, although one South African viper has fangs so long that they jut out of the mouth even at rest.

Vipers are usually shorter than elapids, with much thicker bodies. They are distinguished by large, almost triangular-shaped heads. Vipers can be found almost anywhere from the tropics to near the Arctic Circle. Those that live in colder climates crawl into abandoned mammal burrows in the late fall and hibernate during the winter. Some vipers near the Arctic Circle hibernate up to eight months a year. Occasionally, several snakes and even toads and lizards all share the same hibernating quarters.

The European adder thrives in more locations than any other venomous snake. The phrase "nest of vipers" comes from this snake's mating behavior in which many males will become ensnarled in a writhing mass as they all try to mate with a female. Although venomous, European adders are small and shy and not particularly dangerous.

Far more deadly are the puff adders of central, southern, and western Africa. Puff adders, which live in dry forests and savannahs, cause more human fatalities than any other snake in Africa. These aggressive, bad-tempered snakes derive their common name from their trait of puffing up and hissing loudly when threatened.

Puff adders have such large heads, swollen by poison glands, and thin necks that they resemble a spade or an arrowhead. They are some of the largest, heaviest venomous snakes in the world. Some species can exceed 6 feet (nearly 2 meters) in length. Their fangs are 1½ inch- (3.8-centimeter-) long lances that can bite through leather. Some species can inject enough venom in a single strike to kill five people. Even when it does not kill, the venom may cause permanent tissue damage. The puff adders' hunting technique of burying themselves in debris or lying in ambush, camouflaged against the ground, causes many accidental encounters with humans.

The saw-scaled viper, common in Africa and Asia, grows to only a foot or two (0.3 to 0.6 meters) in length. These snakes are so numerous, well-camouflaged, and aggressive that they cause more bites than any other species in the world. Despite their small size, their toxin effectively stops blood clotting and can cause death by internal bleeding.

Pit vipers   Pit vipers receive their name from a heat-sensing pit between the eyes and nostrils. This organ can distinguish temperature differences of as little as 1 degree Fahrenheit (less than ½ degree Celsius) in its surroundings. Pit vipers use this capability to track down prey by sensing its body heat. Because the pit can detect animals in total darkness, pit vipers often hunt at night.

Most of the 150 or so species of pit vipers live in the Western Hemisphere. An exception is the sharp-nosed viper from the mountain forests of China and Southeast Asia. A common nickname for this snake is the "100-pacer," from the common belief that a victim of its bite can run only 100 paces before dying.

Most cases of venomous snakebites in the United States involve the copperhead. The copperheads' camouflage makes them difficult to see, so hikers and other outdoor enthusiasts often blunder into them. They have small fangs, however, and a venom that works far more effectively against rats and small birds than humans.

An eastern cottonmouth flashes its wide-open mouth in order to scare off predators.

A pit viper with a more fearsome reputation is the water moccasin or cottonmouth. These snakes, which can grow from 3 to 6 feet (1 to 2 meters) long, inhabit swamps, lakes, and rivers from Missouri to Florida.

Unlike most pit vipers, these dullish dark brown snakes will not retreat if disturbed. Instead they try to frighten off their antagonist by opening their wide, white-lined mouths. If not left alone, they may strike repeatedly. Their deadliness is often exaggerated; water moccasins seldom kill people. But their hemotoxin can cause tissue damage so severe that amputation is required.

RATTLESNAKES   Rattlesnakes are the most dangerous of the American pit vipers. North America is home to two dozen species of rattlesnakes. The distinctive rattles at the ends of their tails begin as a single segment. New segments, hollow pieces of a hard material called keratin (the same material that is in fingernails) are added each time the snake sheds its skin, which it does four or five times a year depending on how fast the snake is growing.

No snake in the United States is more deadly than the diamondback rattler. The eastern species of diamondback range from North Carolina to Louisiana. The western diamondbacks live in almost any terrain from Arkansas to California, including 10,000 foot (3,050 meter) mountain peaks.

The size of an eastern diamondback rattler's fang can be judged when it is compared with a match.

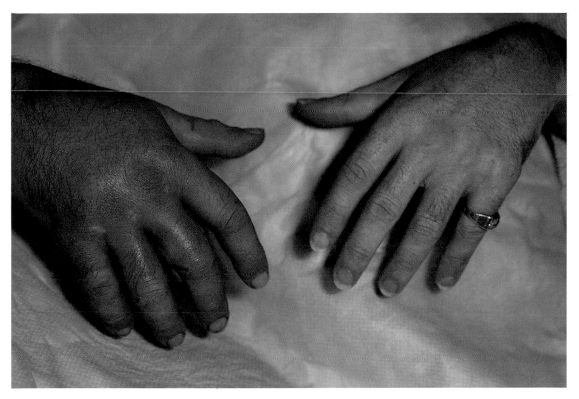

A *snakebite victim's hand still shows the effects of a rattlesnake bite after six days.*

Diamondbacks are named for the design, often outlined in white, that runs down their backs. They may grow to as large as 8 feet (2.5 meters) long. In humans, their hemotoxin breaks down blood cells so that they cannot carry oxygen. If untreated with antivenin, this results in shock, organ failure, and death. Thanks to modern medical treatment, even rattlesnake bites seldom cause tragedy today. Of the 8,000 people bit by rattlesnakes in the United States each year, all but 10 to 12 survive.

SOUTH AMERICAN PIT VIPERS   The largest and most poisonous rattlesnake of all is the bushmaster, which lives in the rain forest lowlands of Central and South America. This snake can grow to 12 feet (3.7 meters) in length, with fangs over an inch (2.5 centimeters) long. Five known cases of bushmaster bites in Costa Rica have resulted in four deaths and one serious injury. Fortunately, people seldom encounter this rare species.

Other dangerous South American pit vipers include the fer-de-lance and the jumping viper. The fer-de-lance has all the characteristics of a lethal snake—large body size, long fangs, aggressive temperament, and highly toxic venom. These yellowish snakes commonly live near waterways in forests and plantations. They cause more fatalities than any other South American snake. The strike of the jumping viper can be especially frightening because it can actually launch its body off the ground. Although only 20 inches (0.5 meters) in length, it can strike prey more than 2 feet (0.6 meters) away.

POISON EVERYWHERE

Poison turns up in some of the most unlikely places in the natural world. There are sponges that store poison. The ocean is home to fire urchins—immobile, plantlike sea creatures with teeth at the end of movable valves. These valves can snap shut, piercing a victim with teeth that can deliver a strong venom. The crown of-thorns starfish is covered with poisonous spines. Even some worms are poisonous.

In fact, poison has proven to be such a useful weapon that virtually all major groups of animals make use of it. Some of the poison-bearing creatures may surprise you.

AMPHIBIANS   Other than the snakes, no other group of vertebrates makes as widespread use of poison as the amphibians. Most frogs, toads, and salamanders have special parotid glands on the head or legs that produce toxin. Amphibians have no way of injecting poison and do not use it to secure food. They simply wear it on their skin.

Poison Dart Frogs   Few animals on earth produce a toxin more deadly than that of the poison dart frogs. This group includes more than 100 species that live in the rain forests, forested mountains, and stream-banks of Central and South America.

Poison dart frogs are tiny, smooth-skinned creatures, rarely as large as 2 inches (10 centimeters) long and frequently measuring only a half inch (1.3 centimeters). They are immediately recognizable by their bright colors, which are often so gaudy they look as though they were painted by a small child. One species, for example, is a brilliant red with shiny blue feet.

Three of these species produce a deadly poison. The most toxic of all, a bright yellow poison dart frog, holds enough poison to kill dozens of people. The toxin acts quickly and interrupts signals between nerves and muscles.

Predators trying to eat one of these frogs experience such a burning pain that they spit out the frog immediately. Even predators that cannot see the frogs have developed ways to avoid eating these amphibious poison pills. Frog-eating bats of South America often zero in on their prey by listening to their mating calls. But these bats are able to distinguish between the high-pitched call of the poison dart frogs and those of more edible frogs. Some other bats that attempt to attack poison dart frogs are able to sense the presence of poison somehow and veer away at the last moment.

Although their colors make them seem cute and appealing, at least three species of poison dart frogs produce deadly toxin.

In 1820 British explorer Captain Charles Cochrane reported an unusual activity among the Choco Indians, who lived on the forested Pacific mountains near the Colombian coast. He described how these South American natives roasted frogs until they "perspire very much." What Cochrane witnessed was the traditional Choco way of obtaining a lethal poison for use with darts. The Choco capture any one of the three most toxic species of poison dart frogs, often by listening for their calls.

When handling these frogs, the Choco protect their hands with leaves. They skewer the frogs onto sharp sticks and heat them over a fire. As the frogs get hot, pores in their skin secrete their toxic mucus, which the Choco rub on their darts. For the most toxic of the poison dart frogs, even this step is unnecessary. The Choco simply pin the frog to the ground with a stick and rub their darts on its back.

Apparently, poison dart frogs manufacture their poison from something in their diet. Those born in captivity do not produce the poison, while those born in the wild continue to be poisonous even in captivity.

Researchers have found evidence that poison may serve as much to protect these frogs from harmful microorganisms as to protect them from predators. In one study frogs quickly died of skin infections after the toxin was removed from their skins.

Toads Frogs are not the only poisonous amphibians. Many toads have poison sacs on their skin, which give them a warty appearance. The poison makes toads taste terrible to predators. The poison can enter a predator's internal system through the roof of its mouth, and may be toxic enough to kill. Toad poison generally effects the blood pressure and heartbeat.

One of the most toxic toads is the marine or cane toad. Originally a native of South America, cane toads were introduced to Australia in 1935 in hopes that they would kill beetles that were destroying the sugarcane crop. The fast-breeding toads have done so well that in parts of the country, the streets stink from road-killed toads.

Cane toads are not dangerous if handled properly, and Australians commonly treat them as pets. But their venom can kill any dog, crow, snake, or even small child that puts one in its mouth. These 4-pound (2-kilogram) amphibians can also shoot poison up to 40 inches (1 meter) when frightened, causing temporary blindness.

Lizards   Only two of the 3,000 species of lizards in the world are poisonous, and both live in Mexico. The most famous is the gila monster, named for its home along the Gila River in the southwestern United States and northern Mexico. Gila monsters can grow up to 2 feet (0.6 meters) long and have large heads and strong claws. They store fat in their thick tails for use when food is scarce. Their scales look much like shiny black and colored beads.

A gila monster's poison glands are located at the rear of the jaw and are connected by ducts to the lizard's grooved teeth. The gila monster is a tena-

Gila monsters make their homes along the banks of the river that gives them their name.

~~ HOTBED OF POISONOUS ANIMALS, PART II ~~

In the Western Hemisphere, Mexico may claim the distinction of having the most impressive array of poisonous animals. This includes more species of venomous snakes than any other country in the Americas; the largest, most deadly rattlesnake; a large variety of dangerous scorpions; and the world's only two poisonous lizards.

cious biter that holds on and chews its highly toxic venom into the victim for up to 10 minutes. About one out of four gila monster bites has been fatal to humans. They bite only when roughly handled, however, and there has never been a confirmed report of a gila monster attack on a human in the wild.

The Mexican beaded lizard is slightly larger and less colorful than the gila monster. Both are nighttime feeders that rely on their sense of smell to find the nests of birds and small mammals on which they prey.

MAMMALS   Mammals are among the least poisonous groups of animals. Yet the platypus of eastern Australia has a venomous hollow spur on the inside of its rear ankles. Venom from this spur can produce severe pain and swelling. A person pierced by this spur may lose the use of a limb for weeks or even months.

No one knows the purpose that this venom serves. Researchers note that only males of the species have venom and that the venom is more powerful during the spring mating season. This has led to speculation that the males may use the poison as a weapon in battles with other male platypusses when courting females.

The only other venomous mammals are small insect-eaters. The common short-tailed shrew has a very weak venomous saliva that may help disable prey. The solenodons of Haiti and Cuba are larger insectivores up to a foot (30 centimeters) long, with tails that may be nearly as long as their bodies. These secretive night hunters, which are nearly extinct, can introduce a venomous saliva with their sharp teeth. Like the shrew venom, it does not appear to have any affect on humans.

The pitohui is the only bird known to be poisonous.

BIRDS   Until the 1990s, ornithologists (scientists who study birds) held up birds as the only major animal group that was completely free of poison. That changed with a discovery by John Dumbacher, a graduate student at the University of Chicago. In 1991 Dumbacher experienced a burning and a numbing sensation when he licked his fingers after handling a pitohui, a bird found in Papua, New Guinea.

Further research showed that the pitohui has poisonous skin, feathers, and organs. Interestingly, the poison is identical to that produced by a species of poison dart frog that has the same orange and black coloring as the pitohui.

POISON—FROM KILLER TO LIFESAVER

The word "poison" almost always triggers a negative reaction. We think of poisons as dangerous, destructive, deadly. People used to label poisons with the sinister skull-and-crossbones, which has recently been replaced by the grimacing "Mr. Yuk." Both symbols indicate that these are substances to be avoided at all costs.

To be sure, poisons can be dangerous and must be treated with care. But there is also a positive side to animal poisons. Not only do these toxins help many creatures survive in a highly competitive natural world, they also provide us with useful health products and valuable information that can relieve suffering and save lives.

Poisons are extremely complex substances. John Daly of the National Institutes of Health has broken down and identified almost 300 different compounds contained in poison dart frog venom alone. Many researchers are now focusing on poisons, trying to unravel some of the secrets that these highly evolved substances contain.

ANTIVENIN RESEARCH   The most logical medical use of animal venom is simply finding antivenins to block the effects of these poisons on the human body.

The production of antivenin is a long and costly process. First, a supply of venom is needed. Getting a poisonous animal to give up its venom is a delicate task that experts refer to as "milking."

Snake milkers, for example, pick up a snake with a long hook and hoist it to their work area. Using tongs to pin the snake down, they force the snake to open its mouth. Then they press the snake's fangs through a plastic covering stretched over a beaker. When the fangs pierce the plastic, the venom flows down into the beaker.

Because snakes secrete only a small amount of poison at any one time, milking a snake produces no more than a few precious drops. Even less venom can be milked from the smallest poisonous animals, such as scorpions and spiders. Therefore, the process must be repeated again and again to produce quantities that medical technicians can work with. Many herpetologists do their milking chores as routinely and regularly as dairy farmers. For example, George Van Horn, founder of the Reptile World Serpentarium in St. Cloud, Florida, has milked up to 90 snakes in a single day.

Next, researchers inject this venom into horses. A horse is able to withstand the injection because it produces a large amount of antibodies that work against the venom. Researchers then extract serum containing these antibodies and concentrate it to create an antivenin that protects humans.

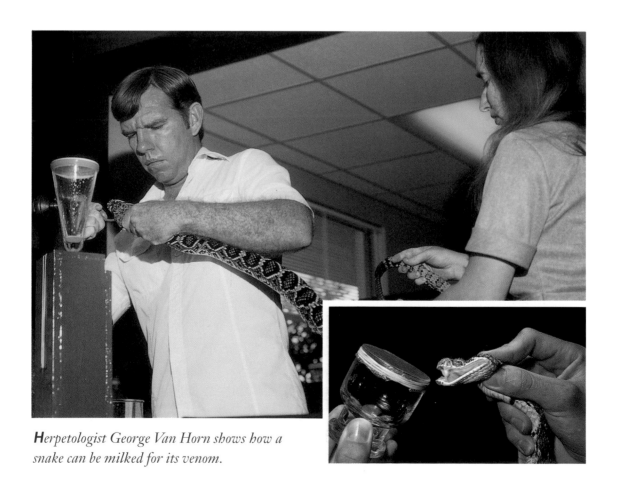

Herpetologist George Van Horn shows how a snake can be milked for its venom.

~ RISKY BUSINESS ~

Those who perform research with venomous animals do so at their own peril. Wild animals are unpredictable, and even the most careful handling of poisonous animals does not guarantee safety.

The most extreme example of this may be Bill Haast, director of the Miami Serpentarium. By 1996 his total number of bites from venomous snakes suffered in the course of his work passed 160. The worst incident involved the notorious saw-scaled viper, whose complex venom is difficult to treat. Haast teetered on the verge of death for a week while doctors injected him with hourly doses of antivenin before he finally pulled through.

Karl Kauffeld, curator for the Staten Island Zoo in New York City, nearly lost his life from a one-fang bite of an Indian cobra. He described the curious effects of the lethal venom: "I felt no pain; it did not even occur to me as strange that the darkness was closing in on the light." Again, massive injections of antivenin saved his life.

Even an experienced, expert snake handler such as George Van Horn recently fell victim to a near-fatal attack. Van Horn had routinely handled thousands of snakes over a career that spanned a quarter of a century and had gone years at a time without a single incident.

But in June of 1995, he lowered his snake hook on the largest of his king cobras. As always when he milked snakes, he wore no gloves because his work required a sensitive touch. Before Van Horn could blink an eye, the cobra struck his arm, then began crawling up the arm, biting as it went.

Van Horn finally shook free of the cobra. Immediately, he gave himself two injections to counteract an allergic reaction that he had developed over the years to snakebites. He was trying to prevent himself from going into anaphylactic shock.

But at the hospital, he slipped into critical condition. His arm swelled to double its size. Doctors delayed injecting him with the tiger snake antivenin that Van Horn provided because they did not know that tiger snake antivenin works well for cobra bites. (The toxins of the two snakes are similar.) More than 50 vials of antivenin were required to save his life. Even after his recovery, Van Horn had to undergo six surgeries and months of rehabilitation to regain use of the arm.

OTHER MEDICAL USES OF VENOM

Innovative research is taking place to determine ways to use the remarkable properties of animal poison to correct a variety of human health problems. For example, neurotoxic venom disables or kills prey by blocking the transmission of nerve signals. Because different types of cone shell venom do this in different ways, scientists use cone shell venom to study the ways in which nerve signals are sent and interrupted. Baldomero Olivera of the University of Utah has been evaluating the toxin of one cone shell species for possible use in the treatment of stroke, a medical emergency that may be caused by too much nerve signal activity.

The ability of hemotoxic venom to stop blood clotting in prey animals has led to studies focusing on the use of this venom to prevent or break up dangerous blood clots in humans.

In this photograph, researchers working with poison dart frogs taste them for poison — something that should definitely be left to the experts!

Toxic chemicals secreted by one type of poison dart frog are being studied for possible use as a painkiller more powerful yet less addictive than morphine. Another poison dart frog toxin shows promise in stimulating the hearts of patients who have suffered heart attacks.

The list of health conditions for which animal venom may provide relief now includes heart disease, arthritis, and multiple sclerosis. It is one of the many ironies of the fantastically complex world of nature that the animal poisons feared by so many may actually do much to improve our lives.

A Brief Guide
to Classification

Because of language differences, animals may be known by various names in different areas of the world. An animal may even be known by more than one name in the same language. For example a puma, a mountain lion, and a cougar are one and the same animal. On the other hand, what many Americans call a buffalo (more properly a bison) is a very different animal from the buffalo of Asia.

The only way scientists all over the world can be sure they are talking about the same living creature is to have a single system of classifying and naming them. The science of classifying and naming animals and plants is called taxonomy. Biologists currently use a system based on the Latin language. It was developed by Swedish scientist Carolus Linnaeus in the eighteenth century. This system allows scientists to group animals and plants together according to their similarities and also to distinguish each organism from all other different organisms.

The broadest classification in the Linnean taxonomic system is the kingdom. Animals belong to the animal kingdom and plants belong to the plant kingdom. Organisms are then grouped according to their phylum. Phyla (plural of phylum) include categories such as Chordata—animals with spinal cords. Organisms within a phylum are further broken down according to class: for example, Chordata includes the class of reptilia, or reptiles. Organisms within a class are then divided according to order: for example, most legless reptiles fall into the order Squamata. Those within an order are next subdivided into a family: for example, the Elapidae family of snakes.

Organisms within a family are further subdivided into genera (plural of genus). For example, the cobras are the genus *Naja*. Those within a genus are divided again according to species: for example, the spitting cobra is a *Naja nigricollis*.

Seven chief groups in the Linnean system of taxonomy, or scientific classification:

KINGDOM

PHYLUM

CLASS

ORDER

FAMILY

GENUS

SPECIES

The text of this book uses common names rather than taxonomic names so that the reader will not be overwhelmed with unfamiliar Latin terms. Taxonomic names for most of the animals cited in the book are listed below. Genus names are always capitalized and italicized. Species names, when used, are lowercase. They follow immediately after the genus name and are also italicized.

ONE

Portuguese man-of-war	*Physalia physalis*
sea wasp (also box jellyfish)	*Chironex fleckeri*

TWO

blue-ringed octopus	*Hapalochlaena maculosa*
cone shells:	
mollusk eaters	*Conus textile* and *C. aulicus*
fish eaters	*C. geographus*, *C. striata*, and *C. purpurascens*
worm eaters	*C. leopardus* and *C. betulinus*

(When writing about an animal, scientists do not write the genus name in full over and over again. Instead, they write it out entirely the first time, and then abbreviate it by giving just the capitalized first letter.)

Asian catfish	*Heteropneustes fossilis*
lionfish (also zebrafish, turkeyfish)	*Pterois antennata, P. lunulata,* and *P. volitans*
	also *Brachirus biocellatus, B. brachyptenus,* and *B. zebra*
man-of-war fish	*Nomeus gronovi*
scat	*Scatophagus argus*
South American catfish	*Pimelodus pictus, P. clarias, P. ornatus,* and *P. albofasciatus*

> **STONEFISH**
> *Synanceia verrucosa*
>
> **KINGDOM:** Animalia
> **PHYLUM:** Chordata
> **CLASS:** Osteichthyes
> **ORDER:** Scorpaeniformes
> **FAMILY:** Synacidae
> **GENUS:** *Synanceia*
> **SPECIES:** *verrucosa*

Toadfish	*Thalassophryne amazonica, T. dowii,* and *T. punctata*

FOUR

bird-eating spider	*Theraphosa blondi*
black widow spider	*Latrodectus mactans*
brown recluse (or fiddleback) spider	*Loxosceles reclusa*
centipedes:	
large tropical species	*Scolopendra subspinipes, S. heros,* and *S. viridicoinis*
large house species	*Scolopendra scutigera*
funnel-web spider	*Atrax robustus*
scorpions:	

Of the five or six families of scorpions, only the family Buthidae contains seriously venomous species. These species belong to the genera *Buthus, Androctonus, Leiurus* and *Buthotus* (Old World) and *Centruroides* and *Tityus* (New World):

(Old World)

Buthus occitanus (Mediterranean)

B. tamulus (India and Pakistan)

Androctonus australis (northern Africa)

A. crassicauda (northern Africa to Middle East)

Leiurus quinquestriatus (northern Africa to Turkey and Middle East)

(New World)

Centruroides exilicauda (Arizona to northern Mexico)

C. vittatus (southeastern United States)

Tityus serrulatus (Brazil)

T. bahiensis (Argentina)

T. trinitatis (Venezuela and Trinidad)

bark (or sculptured) scorpions	*Centruroides exilicauda* and *C. sculpturatus*
Sahara scorpion	*Androctonus australis*

FIVE

African killer bee	*Apis mellifera adansonii*

(Sometimes an animal's scientific name includes its subspecies as well. In this case, *adansonii* is the name of the subspecies. The subspecies name is always given after the genus and species, in lowercase italics.)

assassin bug	
(also wheel bug or kissing bug)	*Arilus cristatus*
bulldog ant	*Myrmecia qulosa*
bumblees	*Bombus lapidarius* and *B. mystacea*
fireant	*Solenopsis invicta*
fire urchins	*Toxopneustes pileolus* and *T. elegans* and *T. roseus*
flannel moth	*Megalopyge opercularis*

HONEYBEE

Apis mellifera

KINGDOM: Animalia

PHYLUM: Arthropoda

CLASS: Insect

ORDER: Hymenoptera

FAMILY: Apoidea

GENUS: *Apis*

SPECIES: *mellifera*

io moth	*Automeris io*
passion vine butterflies	*Heliconius passiflora, H. hecale,* and *H. erato*
tarantula wasp	*Pepsis formosa*

SIX

Australian tiger snakes	*Notechis ater* and *N. scutatus*
boomslang	*Dispholidus typus*
Eastern coral snake	*Micrurus fulvius*
green mamba	*Dendroaspis augusticeps*
king cobra	*Ophiophagus hannah*
kraits	*Bungarus multicinctus* and *B. fasciatus*

pit vipers:

Pit vipers belong to the family Crotalidae, which includes the following genera:

    Crotalus (rattlesnake):

sidewinder rattlesnake	*Crotalus ceraster*

EASTERN DIAMONDBACK RATTLESNAKE
Crotalus adamanteus

- **KINGDOM:** Animalia
- **PHYLUM:** Chordata
- **CLASS:** Reptilia
- **ORDER:** Squamata
- **FAMILY:** Crotalidae
- **GENUS:** *Crotalus*
- **SPECIES:** *adamanteus*

WESTERN DIAMONDBACK RATTLESNAKE
Crotalus atrox

- **KINGDOM:** Animalia
- **PHYLUM:** Chordata
- **CLASS:** Reptilia
- **ORDER:** Squamata
- **FAMILY:** Crotalidae
- **GENUS:** *Crotalus*
- **SPECIES:** *atrox*

Sistrurus (pygmy rattlesnake):
    Mexican pygmy rattlesnake   *Sistrurus ravus*
Bothrops (lance-head snakes):
    fer-de-lance (or barba amarilla)   *Bothrops atrax*
Trimeresurus (Asian lance-head snake):
    Pope's tree viper   *Trimeresurus poporum*
Lachesis:
    bushmaster   *Lachesis mutus*
Agkistrodon:
    copperhead   *Agkistrodon contortrix*
    cottonmouth (or water moccasin) *A. piscivorous*
    sharp-nosed pit viper   *A. acutus*
puff adder   *Bitis arietans*
Russell's viper   *Vipera russelii*
saw-scaled viper   *Echis carinatus*
spitting cobra   *Naja nigricollis*
taipan   *Oxyuranus scutellatus*

SEVEN

cane toad (or marine toad)   *Bufo marinus*
crown-of-thorns starfish   *Acanthaster plancii*
gila monster   *Heloderma suspectum*

PLATYPUS
Ornithorhynchus anatinus
    KINGDOM: Animalia
    PHYLUM: Chordata
    CLASS: Mammalia
    ORDER: Montremeta
    FAMILY: Ornthorhynchidae
    GENUS: *Ornithorhynchus*
    SPECIES: *anatinus*

---

poison dart frogs   *Phyllobates terribilis, P. lehmanni, P. auratus,*
                                  P. histionicus, P. pumilo, P. quinquevittatus and
                                  P. bicolor
solenodon   *Solenodon paradoxa*

GLOSSARY

amphibian   one of a class of animals with backbones distinguished by lack of scales on the body and two stages of development—a larvae with gills to breath in water and adults that breath air; includes frogs, toads, and salamanders

anaphylactic shock   a severe allergic reaction to a foreign substance such as bee or snake venom

antibodies   microscopic agents created by the body to attack and neutralize invading germs and toxins

antivenin   fluid containing antibodies that can be injected into people to protect against the harmful effects of venom

barbel   hairlike projection on the mouth of a fish

chrysalide   casing in which a caterpillar develops into a butterfly

dorsal   situated on or near the back

ectotherm   an animal that obtains body heat from the surrounding environment, a condition commonly called "cold-blooded"

elapid   family of snakes with short, immovable fangs; includes sea snakes, cobras, mambas, taipans, etc.

endotherm   an animal that produces its own body heat, a condition commonly called "warm-blooded"

enzyme   a protein that brings about or aids chemical reactions such as in digestion

filter-feeder   an animal that obtains food by straining small particles suspended in water

hemotoxin   a poison that acts primarily on the blood and tissue

herpetologist   one who studies snakes

icthyologist   one who studies fish

insectivore   an animal that feeds primarily on insects

invertebrate   an animal without a backbone

Jacobson's organ an organ found on the roof of a snake's mouth, used to analyze chemicals in the air to obtain information about other animals in the vicinity

keratin a hard, tough material that makes up fingernails in humans, and rattles in rattlesnakes

maxilliped hooklike appendages under the heads of insects, used to grab and hold food

medusa adult stage of jellyfish

mimicry having a nearly identical appearance to another species of animal. There is usually a survival advantage gained in being mistaken for the other species.

nematocyst specialized capsules in cnidarians that can shoot out a coiled thread with a barbed tip

neurotoxin a poison that acts against the nervous system

nudibranch a type of sea slug

ornithologist person who studies birds

parotid glands salivary glands in the cheek

pectoral located in the chest region

pedipalps enlarged, grasping appendages; pincers

pit vipers vipers that have a heat-sensing pit between the eyes and nostrils

planulae tiny balls of cells, offspring of adult jellyfish

polyp immature form of jellyfish

predator animal that hunts, kills, and eats other animals

prey animal that other animals hunt, kill, and eat

proboscis long, fleshy protrusion in the front or head end of an animal

species in the taxonomy of living things, a group of very closely related organisms

taxonomy the science of classifying animals and plants

telson bulbed portion of a scorpion's tail, contains poison gland

thorax middle section of an insect, between the head and abdomen

toxin poisonous substance

venom poison secreted by animals

vertebrate animal with a backbone

viper family of heavy-bodied, poisonous snakes with long, curved fangs that fold back against the roof of the mouth when not in use

FOR FURTHER READING

Baughman, Lynette. "Encounter With a Desert Killer." *Reader's Digest* (October 1995), 170–176.

Fichter, George S. *Poisonous Animals.* New York: Watts, 1991.

Hamner, W. M. "Australian Box Jellyfish: A Killer Down Under." *National Geographic* (August 1994), 116–130.

Hillyard, Paul. *The Book of the Spider: From Arachnophobia to the Love of Spiders.* New York: Random House, 1994.

Lipske, M. "The Private Lives of Pit Vipers." *National Wildlife* (August 1995), 14–22.

McCafferty, Keith. "The Five Faces of Death." *Field & Stream* (May 1996), 76–78, 114–115.

McDonald, M. *Rattlesnakes.* Danbury, Connecticut: Childrens Press, 1996.

Nichols, John. *Bites and Stings: The World of Venomous Animals.* New York: Facts on File, 1989.

O'Toole, Christopher. *Bees of the World.* New York: Facts on File, 1991.

Shine, Richard. *Australian Snakes: A Natural History.* Ithaca, New York: Cornell University, 1991.

Simon, Seymour. *Snakes.* New York: HarperCollins, 1992.

Thomas, Mike. "Cobra Attack." *Reader's Digest* (December 1995), 128–133.

INDEX

ABOUT THE AUTHOR

Nathan Aaseng attended Luther College in Iowa and earned a B.A. degree with majors in both English and biology. He was particularly interested in the communication of scientific information to general audiences. After working for four years as a microbiologist, he turned to writing full time.

Mr. Aaseng has written more than 100 books, primarily nonfiction for younger readers. He currently lives in Eau Claire, Wisconsin, with his wife and four children.